INTRODUCTION TO FOREX TRADING

A beginner's guide to forex trading

Second edition

Abraham Robert. C

In order to say thank you for purchasing this book, I offer the below video course and more to you as a token of appreciation

__Find the Link to the bonus video courses at the end of the book__

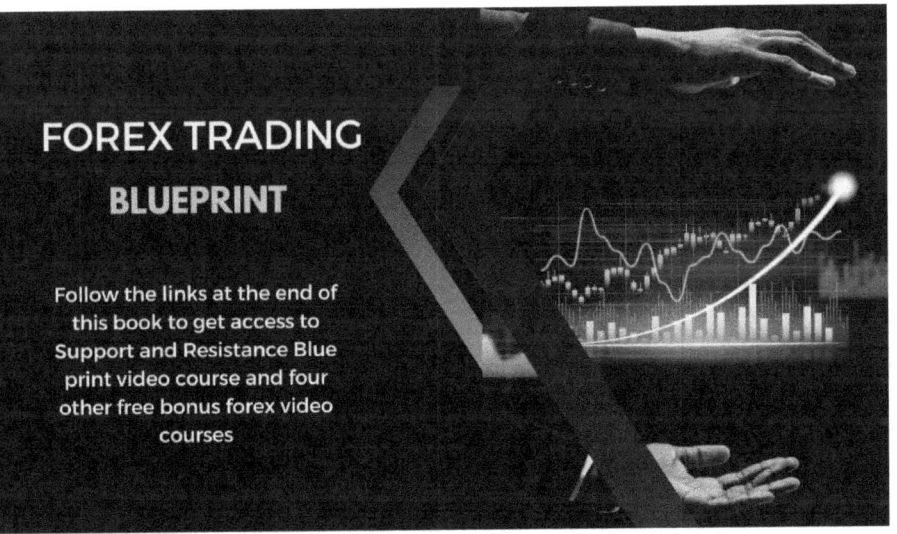

FOREX TRADING
BLUEPRINT

Follow the links at the end of this book to get access to Support and Resistance Blue print video course and four other free bonus forex video courses

TABLE OF CONTENT

CHAPTER ONE

Pullback Strategy in Forex Trading

A brief price reversal or correction against the dominant trend in the financial markets is referred to as a pullback. It happens when a price retreats or retraces from a recent peak (in an upward trend) or low (in a downward trend) with the possibility of a return to the initial path.

Pullbacks are a normal aspect of market dynamics and may be brought on by sellers' momentary imbalances, profit-taking, or changes in market sentiment. Because they expect the underlying trend to resume, traders often see pullbacks as chances to join trades at more favorable pricing.

Trading well during pullbacks needs meticulous research, risk control, and a deep comprehension of market dynamics.

Within the context of a larger trend, traders may benefit from brief market corrections by using the pullback trading method, which is a popular trading tactic. Before the main trend continues, it hopes to benefit from brief reversals.

By identifying and initiating trades during these pullbacks, traders hope to benefit from potential gains when the market realigns with the main trend.

The idea behind the pullback strategy is that markets don't usually move in a straight line. Even in strongly moving markets, there are price retracements when traders take gains or enter into countertrend trades. Those who believe the present trend will continue have trading opportunities during these pullbacks.

How does trading pullbacks work

A pullback is a correction or reversal in prices that takes place within the larger context of a trend.

Its foundation is the idea that markets seldom follow a straight line and often experience brief price retracements before the prevailing trend resumes.

The following is how a pullback trading method is meant to operate:

Identifying the trend

To ascertain the overall trend of the market, traders first look at the price action. This might be a sign of a fall (lower highs and lower lows) or an uptrend (higher highs and higher lows).

Establishing criteria for pullback

Traders determine exactly what constitutes a pullback based on several factors. This might be a return to a particular support level or a percentage decline from a recent peak. Depending on the trader's strategy, time horizon, and tool, the requirements might change.

Waiting for pullback

Traders watch the market carefully and wait for the price to meet their predetermined retreat threshold. They are looking for clues that the present trend could momentarily pause or turn around.

Confirmation and entry

When a pullback occurs and the price satisfies the specified threshold, traders search for confirmation signals that suggest the pullback is about to terminate. Using technical analysis techniques like indicators, chart patterns, or candlestick formations, they validate the possible reversal.

Limitations in trading pullback

False signals

Sometimes pullbacks prove to be misleading signals, which may lead to losses. The market can show a brief reversal that seems to be a retreat, but it might also keep moving in the opposite direction of the initial trend. To increase their chances of success, traders need to use confirmation indications and exercise caution.

Trade exhaustion

When a trend becomes stale or wears out, pullbacks may happen. In these cases, traders who started bets anticipating the trend to continue may lose money since the trend may not return and the price could reverse more sharply.

Difficulty in timing entries

It might be challenging to time the entry point into a pullback trade. Traders need to be able to pinpoint when the trend is going to resume and when the downturn is ending. This calls for careful study and might lead to hurried trade entry or lost opportunities.

Examples of How to use Pullback in Trading

Uptrend Pullback

Find an uptrend in a currency pair by using trend lines or moving averages.

Establish parameters for the decline, such as a 38.2% to 50% retracement of the last rising trend.

Watch for the price to reach the level you have set.

Seek confirmation indicators such as a bullish candlestick pattern or a reversal from a support level.

Make a long transaction (buy) when the price signals the bottom of the decline.

Use a trailing stop-loss or place your profit target at a resistance level to ride the trend.

Downtrend Pullback

Determine whether a currency pair is declining by using trend lines or moving averages.

Establish your criteria for a pullback, which might be a 38.2% to 50% retracement of the recent downward trend.

Watch for the price to reach the level you have set.

Watch for confirmation indicators, including a rejection at a resistance level or a bearish candlestick pattern.

Once the price indicates that the decline is over, do a short sale or short-sell transaction.

Use a trailing stop-loss or place your profit target at a support level to ride the trend.

Reversal versus Pullback

Two distinct ideas exist in trading: pullback and reversal. Below is a summary of how the two vary from one another:

Pullback

A pullback is a brief correction or reversal in price that takes place within the framework of the prevailing trend.

Before the price reverts to its initial path, there is a temporary pullback against the dominant trend.

Pullbacks are seen as chances to join deals at reduced prices in the direction of the trend.

Traders believe that after the retreat is over, the trend will continue.

Pullbacks may be identified using technical analysis techniques including trend lines, moving averages, and Fibonacci retracement levels.

Reversal

Conversely, a reversal indicates a longer-term, more substantial change in the direction of the price trend.

It indicates a total reversal of the existing trend, either up to down or down to up.

Reversals may be identified using certain chart patterns or technical indicators; they are often seen at pivotal levels of support and resistance.

CHAPTER TWO

Categories of Charts

- Time-based
- Price-based
- Activity-based

.

Charts depending on time

The trading chart types that are most frequently utilized are:

Line charts

A line chart forms by joining the closing prices at regular intervals, such as each day in a daily chart.

For longer time periods, such daily or weekly time frames, line charts work really well. At the end of the day or week, the closing prices are important.

You could get blinded by market noise and miss clear support or resistance on a line chart that you would have seen on a candlestick chart.

What are line charts limitations

Reading a line chart makes it easy to overlook information. Because a line chart lacks high and low ranges, it is possible to overlook rising volatility or other significant price levels that are not represented in the closing values.

Bar charts

Bar charts that show the open, high, low, and close (OHLC) as a vertical bar for each session.

Technical analysis using bar charts is a wonderful way to identify levels of support and resistance as well as patterns on the chart, like double tops or head and shoulders.

Bar charts offer the same information as candlestick charts, but some individuals find them visually simpler to detect trends or levels against which the price bounces.

Candlesticks

It show the high and low as "wicks" and the open and closing ranges for each period as a vertical block.

The range between open and close is displayed by the candle's "body," while the high and low points are displayed by the "wicks."

Occasionally, they may be referred to as "Japanese Candlesticks" due to their Japanese origin.

How does time base chart work

The horizontal scale at the chart's bottom will then reflect standard time units when the chart advances according to the time-interval option you select.

The price range for each interval on the chart, for instance, will be represented if you select the daily timeframe. In the event that you select the hourly timeframe, every interval will correspond to one trading hour.

One-minute charts, which often display a day or many days of trade, are a type of time-based chart that can be as short as one-minute intervals of trading. Monthly charts covering decades' worth of price movement across the chart in monthly increments are examples of high periods.

Why use candlesticks instead of bars

The most common kind of trading chart is the candlestick, and many traders only use them.

Candlesticks and bars both display the same information (open, high, low, and close), but traders tend to find candlesticks easier to interpret when identifying price patterns.

For instance, candles that have made significant movement in one direction are simple to identify, particularly if they have opened and closed close to the boundaries of their range.

Charts based on activities

Volume charts

Every candle is created at consistent intervals of volume.

Because inactivity produces fewer candles, it evens out periods of inactivity on volume charts. Many technical analysis methods are still applicable, including moving averages on volume charts and support and resistance.

What are volume charts limitations

Standard volume data is unavailable for markets like spot Forex that lack a centralized exchange. You are depending on volume statistics from Forex futures or your broker, which might not be representative of the entire spot market.

Tick charts

A certain number of ticks or transactions are represented by each candle.

Why use tick charts

Tick charts are perfect for scalpers and short-term traders. When trading on timescales shorter than five minutes, the price may leap around a lot from one period to the next, making the fluctuations somewhat erratic.

Tick charts are a great way to balance it out. You will see fewer candles when there is a prolonged period of inactivity, and more candles when activity comes up.

What are the limitations of using tick charts

Similar to volume charts, standard tick data is absent from markets lacking a centralized exchange. You are depending on data from your broker, which might not be representative of the market as a whole.

Volume profile displays volume transacted at various price points by combining volume and time-based charts.

Volume profile is a time-based chart overlaying a horizontal histogram with the volume traded on the vertical axis.

Why use volume profile

Volume traded at various price points might reveal which levels may prove to be more significant later on and serve as resistance and support.

It provides volume data along with time-based graphics, the best of both worlds.

What are the limitations of using volume profile chart

For volume profiles to be meaningful, historical and precise volume data is required, and in decentralized markets without an exchange, like spot Forex, that isn't always achievable.

Charts based on prices

Range charts

When the price moves inside a given price range, say 100 pip, a candle or bar is formed; the next bar is then formed.

Each bar has the same length and ends at its highest point or lowest point.

Usefulness of Range charts

Range bars are useful for reducing noise. For instance, a range chart will condense the lengthy period of noise that occurs when the price oscillates within a small range into a small number of bars as opposed to showing the entire period as many bars in a standard time-based chart.

What are the limitation of using range charts

Range bars can conceal places where price spends a lot of time and trading activity building up strong support or resistance because they are just dependent on price, not time or volume. This restriction applies to all price-based charts as well.

Point and Figure charts

Columns of Os indicate declining prices, and columns of Xs indicate growing prices.

An "X" is drawn on a point and figure (P&F) chart each time the price increases by a certain amount, or the "box size."

As the price rises, it will keep drawing Xs in the same column.

The price will display a "O" if it drops by a specific amount. But the price needs to change by a certain number of box sizes in order to begin a new column of Os.

Why use P&F charts

Because P&F charts remove a lot of market noise, they can display very clear regions of support and resistance.

False breakout signals can be decreased with P&F charts. When the price breaks out of a level then reverses instead of maintaining its momentum, this is known as a false breakout.

What are the limitations

They may take a while to respond to price changes because a minimum level of movement in price is required before a trend reversal is evident.

How are P&F charts traded?

Point and figure charts can make use of traditional support and resistance.

To learn more about this kind of chart, I suggest checking out some of the P&F chart tutorials that are specifically devoted to it.

Renko charts

These charts resemble a set of bricks that print at predetermined intervals based on how far the price has moved from the preceding brick.

When the market moves more than the brick size away from the previous brick, Renko charts produce a new "brick."

Price activity smaller than the brick size is filtered out by Renko charts.

Renko charts: why use them

Renko charts ignore tiny price movements, which makes them great for emphasizing patterns.

What are the limitations

Renko charts have the ability to conceal places where price and trading activity spend a significant amount of time establishing strong support or resistance because they are only dependent on price, not time or volume. This restriction applies to all price-based charts as well.

When using renko charts, many traditional patterns of technical analysis, like wedges and rounded tops, will not be visible.

Kagi charts

Once the price reverses by a predetermined amount, they reverse course.

The chart will shift when the price reverses and moves by a predetermined amount in the opposite direction.

A kagi chart consists of two lines: the yin line when the price breaks below a previous swing low and the yang line when the price rises above a previous swing high.

Why use Kagi charts

They excel in simplifying the direction of trend highlighting and emphasizing the breakouts of prior highs and lows.

What are the limitations

Because of their unusual design, kagi charts can be challenging to visually grasp and require some practice to utilize.

Since kagi charts only include price and not volume or time, they may obscure periods of high volume or prolonged price movement that are used to establish strong support or resistance. This restriction applies to all price-based charts as well.

CHAPTER THREE

Forex trading timeframes

Any specified period of time during which trading occurs can be referred to as a timeframe in forex trading. Forex timeframes are commonly expressed in terms of minutes, hours, days, or weeks. The timeframe that best fits your trading strategy will be the one you select.

You can begin using timeframe analysis in your forex trading when you've completed your market research and determined which kind of trader you want to be. This will enable you to execute your plan within a set timeframe and open a position during the hours that the currency market is open.

Which timeframe in forex should I trade

Trading techniques and various forex timeframes are directly correlated. However, you must first determine the kind of trader you want to be before you can determine which timeframe is ideal for FX trading.

While some traders, like scalpers, operate over longer time periods, others operate within far shorter timeframes. Your preferred trading technique will determine which forex timeframes are appropriate for you to trade.

The best timeframes in forex for scalpers

Scalping is a trading strategy that entails spotting minute price fluctuations in the foreign exchange market and then making large purchases and sales of currency in brief bursts. Scalpers hope to accumulate a string of little wins that add up to a respectable day's profit by using this approach repeatedly throughout time.

Scalpers typically operate in one- to fifteen-minute time intervals. However, scalpers typically prefer the one- or two-minute intervals.

You can open an account with us after selecting a highly liquid currency pairing in order to implement this technique.

Invest in the market, keep an eye on its movements, and utilize trend analysis to determine the best time to enter the market. After that, you can purchase a specific quantity of the currency of your choice and watch it steadily increase over the course of a minute. When it starts to tick up, you sell your holding, bank the profits, and then repeat the process. You will sell at a slight loss and try again to profit from a new one-minute timeframe if it doesn't move up by the conclusion of the one-minute period.

The best timeframes for forex day traders

The majority of day traders use timeframes ranging from 15 minutes to four hours, reflecting their tendency towards short-term investing.

One advantage of day trading is that you can select from a variety of periods based on your preferred trading technique, the liquidity of the market you've chosen, and the amount of time you have to execute deals.

The best time frame in forex for swing traders

Longer timeframes are typically selected by swing traders so they may take advantage of the benefits of long-term price trend and pattern analysis.

These intervals could extend for a few days, a few weeks, or even several months. To maximize their profits, swing traders may employ stop loss and profit targets, or they may rely on changes in price activity or other technical indicators.

The idea behind swing trading is to profit from an overall price movement over time by keeping an eye on macro trends and utilizing technical analysis to determine the optimal times to enter the market.

This method, which is most effective when applied to less volatile currency pairs, rewards perseverance and market knowledge.

The best time frame in forex for position traders

Position traders, as the name implies, will take a position in a specific forex market and hold it with the expectation that its value would rise over a predetermined time frame. These traders will probably work over very lengthy timeframes, spanning several weeks, months, or even a year, and they won't actually make many deals.

Position traders don't only store their money in an account for the foreseeable future, in contrast to standard "buy and hold" investors.

They are followers of trends, and their goal is to spot a trend, invest in it, and then sell off when the trend peaks.

How to conduct analysis across several timeframes

In order to identify as many trading opportunities as possible, multiple timeframe analysis looks at a specific currency pair simultaneously over a number of distinct time periods.

The majority of traders will first select two timeframes: one longer and one shorter. When conducting multiple timeframe analysis, traders typically utilize a ratio of 1:4 or 1:6, using a four- or six-hour chart as the longer timeframe and a one-hour chart as the lower timeframe.

While the shorter timeframe can be used to pinpoint the best places to enter the market, the longer duration can be utilized to spot trends. The market trends can then be examined in greater detail by adding a third, medium-term timeframe.

You may manage multiple trading positions at once with the aid of multiple timeframe analytical techniques, all without raising your risk profile. This trading technique can potentially benefit from the usage of indicators.

CHAPTER FOUR

TRADING SESSIONS

What is a Trading Session?

An asset's or a location's active trading hours are referred to as a trading session. A market's single trading day is the trading session that investors in that market refer to. Generally, different markets have distinct trading hours.

Understanding Trading Sessions

Around the world, different asset classes adhere to various trading session hours. On weekdays, the U.S. bond market trades from 8:00 a.m. to 5:00 p.m. EST, whereas the trading session for U.S. equities begins at 9:30 a.m. and concludes at 4:00 p.m. EST.

The American stock market ends for the week at 1:00 p.m. EST, whereas the American bond market shuts at 2:00 p.m. EST on weekdays. Different trading sessions are held in the futures market based on the public exchange and commodity being traded.

Traders should be informed of the opening and closing times of the assets they are trading in order to arrange their trading hours, as different asset classes have distinct trading periods.

Trading sessions before the market and after hours

Even though some markets only have official trading hours throughout the day, several have extended their trading hours to include pre-market and after-hours trading due to rising trading demand and the use of electronic trading.

For instance, the NYSE is normally open from 9:30 a.m. to 4:00 p.m., but on weekdays, pre-market trading begins at 4:00 a.m. and ends at 9:30 a.m. EST, and after-hours trading continues until 8:00 p.m.

Nonetheless, different exchanges and nations may have different pre-market and after-hours trading hours.

Traders can profit from announcements and company news released outside of usual trading hours thanks to the extended trading hours. To prevent producing volatility in stock prices during trading hours, for instance, the majority of publicly-traded corporations release their earnings either before or after the market opens. It enables investors to respond to news quickly even before the market opens—and outpace other investors who hold off on trading until the market opens.

The advent of electric trading systems and other private trading systems has made pre-market and after-hours trading available to all investors, even if extended trading was previously only available to institutional and high-net-worth investors.

24-Hour Trading Session

Certain marketplaces allow trading to occur around-the-clock. One market that is open for trading twenty-four hours a day is the foreign currency market. Large banks and brokerage houses that deal in many currency pairs, including the USD, GBP, NZD, JPY, etc., make up the foreign exchange market.

Sunday night marks the start of the FX market, which closes on Friday night, making five trading days a week. Even though the market is open for business around the clock, investors only trade during a few hours during which there are significant market moves.

Alternatively, rather than trying to trade all day, traders might concentrate on trading during the three main trading sessions: the London Session, the New York Session, and the Tokyo Session.

Asian Session (GMT 22:00–08:00)

Sydney open (22:00 GMT) and Tokyo close (08:00 GMT) mark the start and finish of the Asian session.

Despite the fact that we refer to it as the Tokyo session, Japan is the third-largest forex trading hub in the world. However, there are other bustling forex hubs during this time. Sydney, Singapore, and Hong Kong are also significant players in this.

Naturally, the yen is the most traded currency, accounting for 16.5% of all forex transactions.

Let's now examine the principal elements of this session:

This session handles about 21% of all FX transactions.

Sometimes there can be very little liquidity, or currency sold without creating noticeable price fluctuations.

Most currency pairings will trade inside a range due to this minimal liquidity, particularly if there was a significant move in the previous New York session.

Since economic news is provided at the start of the session, this is when most activity occurs.

Pairs containing JPY, AUD, and NZD are anticipated to experience larger moves as economic news from Australia, New Zealand, and Japan is released throughout the Asian session.

London Session (08:00-16:00 GMT)

Despite the fact that there are other financial hubs around Europe, London is the primary financial Centre and is regarded as the capital of FX. It makes sense given that the London session:

Has a large trading volume (this session handles more than 32% of all FX transactions).

Possesses great liquidity

Is when most market uptrends and downtrends occur.

Possesses smaller spans

Because most traders are off for lunch, volatility (i.e., overall price changes) slightly decreases in the middle of the London period until the start of the New York trading session.

Occasionally, just before the session closes, market patterns may turn around when European traders choose to lock in their winnings.

New York session: 13:00–21:00

The New York (US) session begins when the traders from the London session return from lunch.

The following characteristics set apart the US session:

This is where about 19% of all currency transactions are completed.

High potential to move the market: USD is used in 85% of deals.

Lots of liquidity in the early morning when it falls within the London session

The majority of economic news releases occur early in the session.

In the afternoon, volatility and liquidity both decline.

There was minimal movement on Friday afternoon, with a strong likelihood of a trend reversal in the latter part of the day.

CHAPTER FIVE

TRADING METHODS

Scalping

The shortest term kind of trading is scalping. Scalp traders seldom keep open positions more than a few minutes or seconds. These brief transactions aim to capture minute intraday price changes. The idea is to execute a large number of rapid transactions with lesser profit margins in order to build up profits over the course of the day from the volume of deals made during each trading session.

Tight spreads and liquid markets are necessary for this trading strategy. Because of the huge trading volume and liquidity of key currency pairings like EURUSD, GBPUSD, and USDJPY, scalpers often trade exclusively these pairs.

Additionally, they frequently trade just at the busiest periods of the trading day, when there is higher trading volume and frequently volatility during the overlap of trading sessions. Because they enter the market so frequently, scalpers seek out the tightest spreads available because paying a greater spread would reduce their prospective gains.

Given that you will need to focus on charts for several hours at a time, the fast-paced trading environment of trying to scalp a few pips as many times as possible throughout the trading day may be extremely time-consuming and unpleasant for many traders. Scalpers often trade one or two pairs because the activity may be rather strong.

Day trading

Day trading might be suitable for individuals who are uneasy with the rigors of scalping but still don't want to keep holdings overnight.

Unlike swing and position traders, day traders begin and leave their positions on the same day, eliminating the possibility of any significant overnight movements.

They conclude their trade with a profit or a loss at the conclusion of the day. Because trades are often maintained for a few minutes or hours, it is necessary to have enough time to evaluate the markets and regularly check positions throughout the day. Day traders, like scalpers, depend on regular little wins to increase their earnings.

Swing trading

Swing traders normally maintain positions for several days, sometimes even for a few weeks, in contrast to day traders who hold positions for less than a day.

Traders do not have to spend the entire day watching the charts and their transactions because positions are kept for a while to take advantage of brief market movements.

Because of this, it's a well-liked trading technique among those who want to trade in their free time but have other obligations (like a full-time work). Still, setting aside a few hours each day to examine the markets is essential.

Trading techniques including trend, countertrend, breakout, and momentum trading are frequently employed by swing traders as well as certain day traders.

Position trading

Position traders seek to maximize possible earnings from significant market swings by concentrating on long-term price movement. Trades therefore typically take place over the course of several weeks, months, or even years. Weekly and monthly price charts are frequently used by position traders to study and assess the markets. They combine technical and fundamental research to determine possible entry and exit points.

Position traders should just periodically monitor their positions to maintain an eye on the main trend, as opposed to regularly monitoring their positions as they would other trading methods since they are not concerned with little price variations or pullbacks.

Risk management in foreign exchange mean

You may put in place a set of guidelines and controls using forex risk management to make sure that any unfavorable effects of a deal are under control. Planning ahead is essential for an effective strategy since it is preferable to have a risk management strategy in place prior to trading.

Risk that comes with trading forex

• **Risk associated with currency**

This is the risk connected to currency price fluctuations, which can make purchasing overseas assets more or less expensive.

- **Risk associated with interest rates**

is the risk associated with an abrupt change in interest rates, which has an impact on volatility. Interest rate movements have an impact on foreign exchange rates because they can influence expenditure and investment levels to rise or fall across an economy.

- **Risk associated with liquidity**

Risk associated with liquidity is the chance that you won't be able to purchase or sell an item fast enough to stop a loss. Despite being a very liquid market, there may be times when it is not, depending on the currency and the government's foreign exchange regulations.

- **Leverage risk**

Leverage risk is the possibility of compounding losses while using margin to trade. It's simple to underestimate how much money you are risking because the initial investment is less than the FX trade's worth.

- **Social Risk**

Social risk and the social problems that exist in a certain nation are related. This covers the possibility of societal instability as well as political, economic, and social problems. Selecting a broker from a nation whose reputation you can trust as well as its political and economic stability can help to reduce social risk.

Countrywide Risk

This is the danger that comes with dealing in a certain currency within a particular nation. This includes the danger of depending on a middleman in a nation dealing with political and economic unrest. Making sure you have a suitable broker in a nation you have investigated and determined to be politically and economically stable will help to lessen this.

Legal Risk

This kind of risk entails breaking trade regulations within a nation. This may entail actions like passing legislation and regulations. It is your responsibility as a forex trader to confirm that your broker is licensed in order to adhere to national regulations. By working with a licensed broker who possesses the necessary licenses, this can be lessened.

Risk in Operations

This is a risk related to your trading platform's infrastructure and technology. This usually covers elements like the trading platform's dependence on external networks and the caliber of the trading programe. Examining the safety aspects of the broker before trading with them will help to lessen this.

Possible Advantages Forex Risk Management Offer

1. Conserve funds

You may reduce your financial loss by using risk management techniques. In this manner, it will be much easier for you to handle any changes in currency pairings. Many organizations are unaware that using FX risk management solutions might help them reduce the risk to which they are exposed. The crucial information is that they are meant to reduce, not entirely eliminate, the currency risk you are exposed to, so you will not incur losses that you may have otherwise.

2. Risk of Diversity

One popular tactic in risk management measures is risk diversification. To put it simply, diversification is the act of not placing all of your money into a single currency pair. You may be susceptible to changes in the value of that currency pair if you are trading only that one pair. However, since you are not exposed to a single currency pair when you trade in numerous currencies, you are less susceptible to currency risk.

Forex Risk Management Techniques

Now that you are aware of the dangers associated with forex trading, you should also be aware of the techniques for managing your trade risk. Although these tactics might differ from trader to trader, they always aim to reduce the effects of risk.

It's crucial to remember that you may use risk management techniques to assist you prevent significant losses. The following are a few of the most often used techniques for managing FX risk:

1. Put Stop Loss Orders to Use

Using a stop-loss order can assist you prevent significant losses in the event that your transaction is unsuccessful. Stop-loss orders are applicable to both long and short transactions, and you may adjust the stop loss to suit your own trading style.

Make the most of your investments and steer clear of those huge losses that can endanger your trading account with the aid of a solid stop-loss order.

2. Employ Stop Loss Order Trailing

Having a trailing stop-loss order is crucial if you are a short-term trader. Trailing stop-loss orders might assist you maximize your trade and diversify your revenue stream if you want to retain your position for a little length of time.

A stop-loss order that is utilized to close the gap between your entry point and your stop loss is known as a trailing stop-loss order. This tactic can assist you in reducing your losses.

3. Verify That You Are Correctly Capitalized

Recall that investing in FX is quite dangerous. If, however, you are not well capitalized, this is not the investment for you. Examining your capitalization before you begin trading is crucial. This will assist you in obtaining the necessary funds to apply these tactics successfully.

4. Easily Recognize Your Trades

Making the most of your investment and assessing your risk may be achieved by identifying your transactions early. Making early trade identifications increases the likelihood that you can reduce your losses through careful preparation.

5. Be Ready to lose Money

When trading in the forex market, there is always a chance that you might lose money, no matter how hard you work at it. Recall that before you begin trading, you should have a set amount of money that you are willing to lose.

6. Employ Limit and Stop Orders

Orders for stop and limit can be used to assist you control your risk, even if they aren't strictly risk management tactics. This is because you can successfully control your trades and establish your degree of risk if you utilize this kind of order. In this manner, you may maximize your trading profits.

7. For long positions, use a margin

You will require a method to control the risks as you take on lengthier holdings. The majority of forex trading platforms always have margin available. If you have a strong belief in your trade, this is an excellent method for you to manage your risks. You may maximize your investment by doing this.

8. Blend Various Techniques

To maximize your trading profits, it is crucial to combine any several tactics you may have at your disposal. It is imperative that you ensure the tactics you employ are appropriate for your situation.

9. Make Use of a System That Suits You

Developing a risk management approach that is appropriate for you requires that you design your own system. When you are initially starting out, it is crucial to make sure you have the proper knowledge and are using the appropriate resources before you begin developing your own plan.

GET INSTANT ACCESS TO THE FREE VIDEO COURSE BY FOLLOWING THE BELOW LINK

subscribepage.io/freeforexcourse

Click or copy and paste the above link on your browser for instant access to the bonus video.

Happy Trading!